a smart girl's guide

Staying
Home Alone

a girl's guide to feeling safe and having fun

by Dottie Raymer
illustrated by Julie Douglas

Published by American Girl Publishing
Copyright © 2009, 2015 American Girl

Questions or comments? Call 1-800-845-0005,
visit **americangirl.com**, or write to Customer Service,
American Girl, 8400 Fairway Place, Middleton, WI 53562-0497.

Printed in China
15 16 17 18 19 20 21 LEO 10 9 8 7 6 5 4 3 2 1

Editorial Development: Teri Robida, Elizabeth Ansfield, Elizabeth A. Chobanian,
Michelle Watkins, Carrie Anton, Laurie Zelinger, Ph.D., M.S., RPT-S
Art Direction and Design: Lisa Wilber
Production: Jeannette Bailey, Tami Kepler, Judith Lary, Paula Moon, Kristi Tabrizi
Illustrations: Julia Bereciartu

Special thanks to: Molly Kelly, American Red Cross, Badger Chapter
David A. Riley, Ph.D., University of Wisconsin–Madison

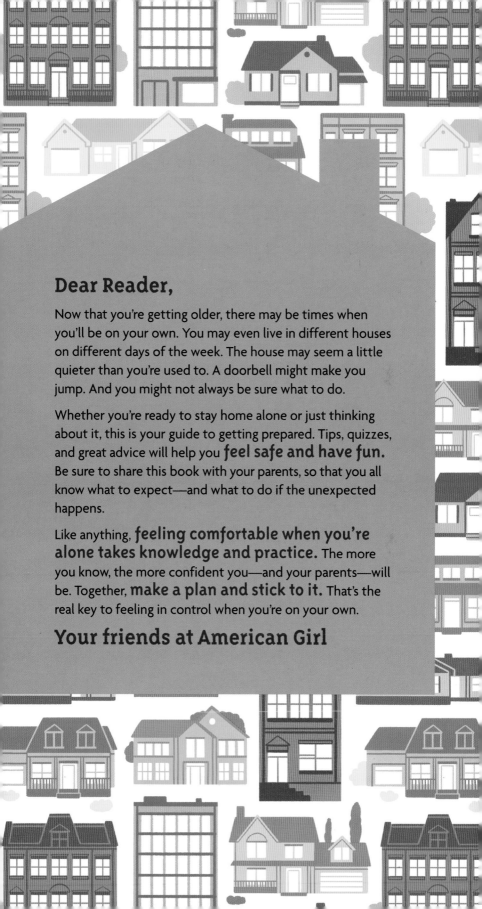

Dear Reader,

Now that you're getting older, there may be times when you'll be on your own. You may even live in different houses on different days of the week. The house may seem a little quieter than you're used to. A doorbell might make you jump. And you might not always be sure what to do.

Whether you're ready to stay home alone or just thinking about it, this is your guide to getting prepared. Tips, quizzes, and great advice will help you **feel safe and have fun.** Be sure to share this book with your parents, so that you all know what to expect—and what to do if the unexpected happens.

Like anything, **feeling comfortable when you're alone takes knowledge and practice.** The more you know, the more confident you—and your parents—will be. Together, **make a plan and stick to it.** That's the real key to feeling in control when you're on your own.

Your friends at American Girl

contents

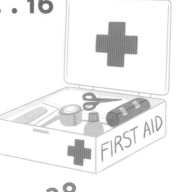

boredom busters . . . 42

stay in control . . . 52

good for you! . . . 62

Use the house-rules workbook to help you—and your family—keep track of need-to-know info.

are
you
ready?

key thought

talk it over

Get together with your parents. Talk over any questions you have, and find out what's expected of you. The more information you have, the more prepared you'll be.

ready or not?

Are you calm in a crisis? Or do sticky situations catch you off guard? How you handle the unexpected will give you an idea of how comfortable you'll feel by yourself. Take this quiz to find out.

1. You and your mom are shopping for back-to-school clothes. You turn around to show your mom a shirt, and she's not there! You . . .
   a. keep shopping. She'll catch up with you sooner or later.
   b. stay where you are. It's where she last saw you, so it'll be the first place she'll look when she discovers you've been separated.
   c. run through the store shouting, "Mom! Mom! Where are you?"

2. You wake up in the middle of the night and see a strange shadow in the corner of your room. You . . .
   a. tell yourself it's just your imagination, and go back to sleep.
   b. turn on the light to make sure it really is just your bathrobe on the back of your chair.
   c. call out to your parents.

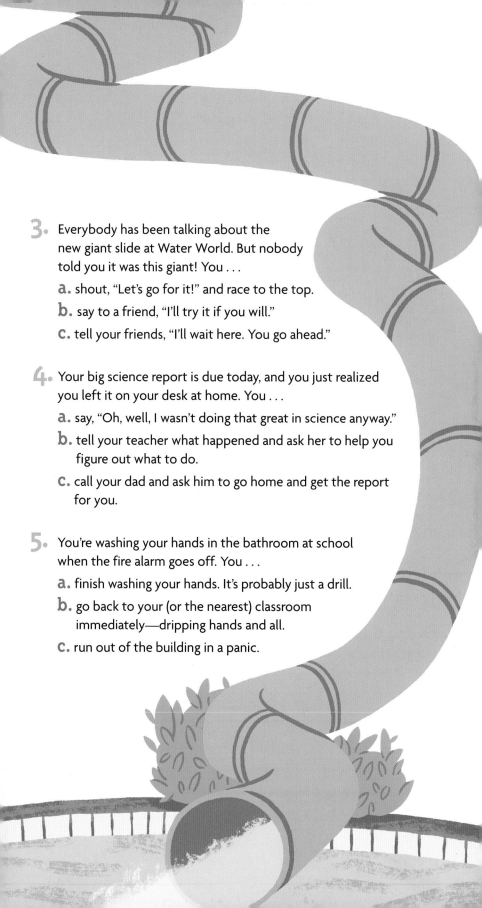

3. Everybody has been talking about the new giant slide at Water World. But nobody told you it was this giant! You . . .

a. shout, "Let's go for it!" and race to the top.

b. say to a friend, "I'll try it if you will."

c. tell your friends, "I'll wait here. You go ahead."

4. Your big science report is due today, and you just realized you left it on your desk at home. You . . .

a. say, "Oh, well, I wasn't doing that great in science anyway."

b. tell your teacher what happened and ask her to help you figure out what to do.

c. call your dad and ask him to go home and get the report for you.

5. You're washing your hands in the bathroom at school when the fire alarm goes off. You . . .

a. finish washing your hands. It's probably just a drill.

b. go back to your (or the nearest) classroom immediately—dripping hands and all.

c. run out of the building in a panic.

6. Your dad is 15 minutes late picking you up from soccer practice. You . . .

   a. walk to the nearest store and buy a can of soda. At least you won't die of thirst while you wait.

   b. stay at your pickup point and dig a book out of your backpack to pass the time.

   c. worry that he forgot to pick you up and ask a friend's mom for a ride.

7. Your aunt gives you a new camera for your birthday. But you need to learn how to use it before you snap any pictures. You . . .

   a. toss aside the directions and figure out how to work it yourself.

   b. dive into the directions. If you have any questions, you'll ask your mom.

   c. give the directions to your mom. Once she's read them, she can teach you.

Answers

Daring Daisy

If you answered mostly a's, you've probably been feeling ready to stay home alone for a while now. You're easygoing and feel sure you can handle any challenge that comes your way. But sometimes you may be too quick to respond. Slow down. Take some time to think before you act. Thinking things through will help you make good decisions on your own.

Reliable Rose

If you answered mostly b's, you are capable and reliable—two great qualities! You're probably ready to stay home by yourself, but you may still be feeling a little uncertain. Perhaps you're worried that you'll have too much responsibility, or that you'll get lonely or bored. Talk with your parents about what is worrying you. Together, you can figure out what you need to feel comfortable with the new arrangement.

Panicky Petunia

If you answered mostly c's, you may like the idea of staying home alone but easily get the jitters. Or you're not sure about the idea at all but may not have a choice. Why not try a couple of test runs first—say, while your parents run an errand or visit with a neighbor. If you still don't feel ready, tell your parents how you feel and talk about finding an alternative. Your school counselor can tell you about other options that are available in your area.

house rules

Different families have different rules. Talk with your parents about your family's house rules. That way, you'll all know what to expect about what you can—and can't—do when you're home alone.

Check In

You get home, lock the door behind you, and then what? You probably need to check in with an adult to let him or her know you got home. Ask your parents who you should check in with and how.

Hel-lo?

What should you do when the home phone rings? Do you answer it? Let the call go to voicemail or the answering machine? Should you check messages? If you answer the phone, what do you say? Is there a time limit on calls to friends on your cell or home line?

Ding-Dong!

The best house rule is not to answer the door at all. If you have a short list of people you can allow in when you're alone, come up with a system so that you know who's at the door before you open it.

Net-Wise

Are you allowed to e-mail friends? Check certain websites? Enter chat rooms? Surf the Internet? Find out how your parents feel about you logging onto your computer or smartphone when you're home alone.

Home Turf

For some girls, "home" means "in the house." For others, it means "in the yard" or "in the neighborhood." Ask your parents what your home territory is.

Snack Time

What are you allowed to snack on when you get home? Can you make it yourself? Are any foods or appliances off-limits?

On Schedule

Do homework . . . or play with the cat? Shoot baskets . . . or clean your room? Your parents might have one opinion. You might have another. Talk about it, and work out a suitable schedule.

golden rules

Even though every family has different rules, some basic rules apply to everyone. Follow these golden rules, and you'll feel—and be—in control!

Always lock the door.

Believe it or not, leaving your key in the door by accident is an easy thing to do. Avoid this mistake by forming a good habit. As soon as you walk in the door, put your key in a special spot, such as on a hook or in a dish. Make it the first thing you do after you shut and lock the door behind you.

Check in.

Always let your parents know where you are. Call to keep your parents up-to-date if your schedule changes one day or is so busy that it gets confusing. And always check with a parent before you change your plans.

Never tell anyone you're alone.

You can be polite without letting people know you're alone. If someone calls for your mom, ask for a name: "Who are you trying to reach?" Ask who's calling, and then say, "She's busy right now. I'll let her know you called," and hang up.

Trust your instincts.

If you're uncomfortable about a situation, pay attention to that gut feeling. Your instincts help keep you alert. If something doesn't seem right—the walk home, a neighbor, a stranger, anything—call your parents. It's never silly to listen to those "funny feelings."

Never let anyone in the house.

Your best bet is to never unlock the door and never let anyone in the house. Ignoring the doorbell isn't rude if it keeps you safe. Talk to your parents about specific rules for your house.

Have a backup plan.

No matter how prepared you are, accidents sometimes happen. Whether you've lost your key, missed the bus, or forgotten your homework at school, you need to have a backup plan when something goes wrong. Talk to your parents about what to do—and who to turn to for help—when things don't go according to plan.

key thought

know where things are

Knowing where something is at the time you need it—whether it's your house key or a cell phone—will keep you safe and in control.

pocket power

Before you leave your house, make sure you have what you need to get home safely. Keep these VIPs—Very Important Possessions—tucked safely inside a pocket in your backpack or a pocket in your clothes.

Quick Snack
You can't think straight when you're hungry. An extra granola bar or a piece of fruit will keep away those hunger pangs until you get home.

Money
Have the exact change you'd need to ride the bus.

Emergency Numbers

Have your parents' work or cell numbers and other emergency numbers programmed into your cell phone. You should also have them handy on a wallet-sized card in case your cell-phone battery dies.

Phone

Carry along a cell phone or have money to make a call on a pay phone.

House Key

Don't hang it on your belt or backpack strap for anyone to see. Hide it away, safe and sound.

know your neighborhood

Chances are, you're pretty familiar with your neighborhood. If your parents don't live together, you might even know two different neighborhoods. But think about it: Do you know the safe places you can go—and the not-so-safe places you need to avoid? Here are some things to look for the next time you take a walk around the block:

Public Places

Small neighborhood businesses or community centers are good places to go when you're in a jam, especially if you see kids inside.

Street Names

Know the name of the cross street nearest to your house. If you call an emergency number, the operator might ask you for this information.

Safe Spots

Steer clear of places, such as alleys, empty buildings, or lonely lots, that make you feel uncomfortable. If you live in an apartment building, elevators or staircases may make you feel uneasy, too. Wait for someone you trust to join you before you go up or down.

Pay Phone

If you don't have a cell phone, knowing where to make a call means you're one step closer to getting help. If there are no pay phones in the area, go to a friendly neighbor's house to use the phone.

Friendly Neighbor #1

Is there a trusted neighbor home during the day? If so, ask your mom to give her a spare house key.

Friendly Neighbor #2

Have a backup person to turn to for help, just in case the person you usually would go to isn't home.

key care

Where would you be without your house key?
Locked out, that's where! Take good care of your
key, and it'll take care of you.

- **DON'T** hide an extra key outside your house.
  Police say that burglars know all the good hiding
  places, too!

- **DON'T** lend your key to anyone—not even
  a friend.

- **DON'T** write your name or address
  on the key. You don't want
  to give a stranger a written
  invitation to your house!

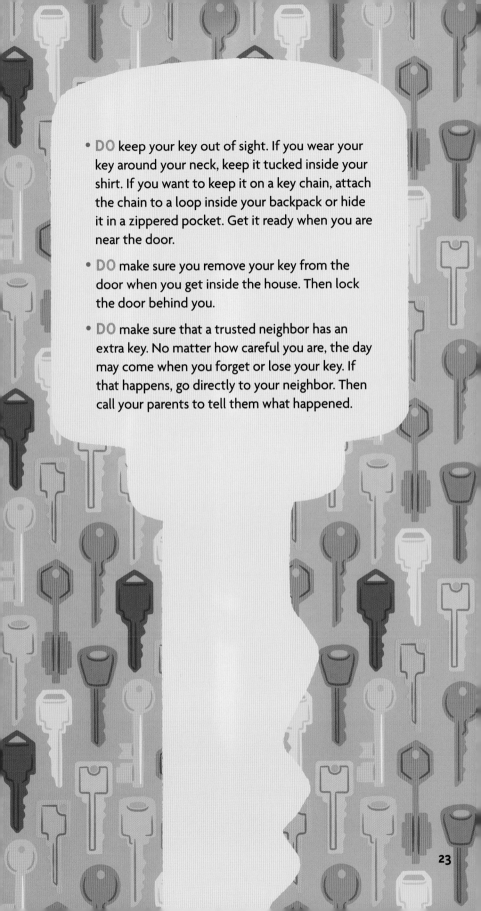

- **DO** keep your key out of sight. If you wear your key around your neck, keep it tucked inside your shirt. If you want to keep it on a key chain, attach the chain to a loop inside your backpack or hide it in a zippered pocket. Get it ready when you are near the door.

- **DO** make sure you remove your key from the door when you get inside the house. Then lock the door behind you.

- **DO** make sure that a trusted neighbor has an extra key. No matter how careful you are, the day may come when you forget or lose your key. If that happens, go directly to your neighbor. Then call your parents to tell them what happened.

got it?

A good set of supplies will help you feel confident and in control! Make sure you know where everything on this list is kept.

Family Calendar

If you have a smartphone, use the family calendar app to keep track of schedules. Or hang a large calendar on the wall at home. Get into the habit of jotting your schedule on the calendar. Get others in your family into the same habit so that you know where they will be, too.

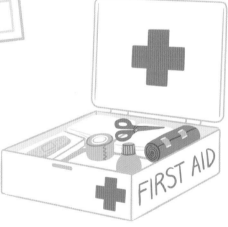

First-Aid Kit

You can buy a complete kit at a pharmacy. Or you and your parents can make your own. Call the Red Cross or a local hospital to find out what items to include in the kit.

Emergency Phone Number List

Make sure your parents' phone numbers and all other emergency numbers are entered into your cell phone. Even if you have a cell phone, use the pull-out booklet in the back of this book to keep track of the numbers you need.

Cell-Phone Charger

If your cell-phone battery is running low, charge it as soon as you get home.

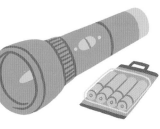

Flashlight with Extra Batteries

Never use candles or matches when you are home without an adult.

Message Board

A dry-erase board or a bulletin board will keep your family's lines of communication open. If the board is next to the telephone, so much the better! If not, make sure there is a notepad handy for phone messages.

Emergency Fund

Keep $20 in cash, plus change for a pay phone, in a safe place. And remember— no borrowing from the emergency fund for ice cream!

Battery-Operated Radio

This radio is for emergencies, not for listening to your favorite tunes! If your electricity goes out in a storm, the radio will come in handy for weather bulletins.

home sweet home

You want to feel comfortable when you're home by yourself—and you can. That comfort starts with knowing that your house is as safe as can be. See how many of these things you can find:

- Dead-bolt locks
- Smoke and carbon monoxide detectors (at least one of each on each floor)
- Outside lights
- Peephole in front door
- List of emergency numbers by the phone
- Closed windows with locks
- First-aid kit on a shelf in the bathroom
- Flashlights on a shelf in the kitchen and on each floor of the house

Is your house missing anything on the list? If so, talk to a parent about it.
The more things you can check off, the more prepared you'll be.

coming home

key thought

use your head

Making good choices starts with using
your own best judgment. Take the
time to think things through,
and you won't go wrong.

it's your choice

When you walk in the door, you have lots of choices to make. What are your at-home habits?

1. You put your house key . . .
  a. somewhere in your room.
  b. in a special spot by the front door.
  c. in the pocket of your jeans.

Tucking your key in your jeans or stashing it somewhere in your room means you'll have to hunt for it before you leave for school the next morning. You may even end up losing it! Make a habit of putting your key in the same spot every day.

2. Your coat goes . . .
  a. in the closet.
  b. over a chair.
  c. on the floor.

It's easy to toss your coat on a chair or leave it on the floor. But if you put things away to begin with, you won't have to clean up later. Hang up your coat in the closet.

3. You make a call to . . .
  a. get the homework assignment from a classmate.
  b. check in with Mom.
  c. chat with a friend.

Let one of your parents know that you're home before you do anything else. After that, follow the house rules for talking on the phone.

4. You snack on . . .
  a. a candy bar.
  b. soda and chips.
  c. milk and a bagel.

Candy, soda, and chips give you energy fast, but it doesn't last. Grab a good-for-you snack instead. Make a list of healthy options with your parents and put it on the fridge for quick reference.

5. You sit down to . . .
  a. do your homework.
  b. play a video game.
  c. watch TV.

You can easily lose track of time when you turn on the TV or play a game. The sooner you start your homework, the sooner it will get done.

i'm not scared ... am i?

Everybody feels scared at times. It's your body's way of keeping you alert and ready to take action. Tell a parent or other adult how you feel. They can help you take control of your fear.

Where's My Mom?

Your mom is usually home by 5:30. But it's 6:00, and she's not home yet. You know she's probably still at work, but you can't help worrying.

Work out a system for Mom to let you know when she's going to be late. Make sure you and she agree on what "late" means—five minutes after she's expected, fifteen minutes, half an hour? Know who to call when your mom is late and can't be reached.

What's That Noise?

You're doing your homework when you hear the floor creak downstairs. Your heart begins to thump. Is somebody there? Or is it just your imagination?

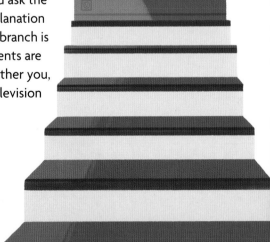

Tame those noises that make you nervous by getting to know them. Go on a noise hunt with an adult. Make a list of the sounds, and ask the adult to help you find an explanation for each noise. Maybe a tree branch is hitting a window, or the air vents are creaking. If the noises still bother you, try turning on the radio or television to drown them out.

It's Too Dark!

You hate October. That's when it gets dark early. And coming home to a dark, empty house gives you the creeps!

Tell your parents how you feel. They can install a light timer so that one or two lights will be on when you get home from school. They can also ask a neighbor to turn on an outside light when it begins to get dark. After you lock the door behind you, turn on all the lights you need to feel comfortable, and close the curtains. And if there's a room in your house that feels particularly dark, put an extra light or nightlight there, too.

sibling struggles

Brothers and sisters—sometimes they're your best friends, and other times you'd rather be alone. It's not always easy to get along. But the key to good relationships is communication. Talking things over with your siblings and your parents can help.

Who's in Charge?

When you're home by yourselves, your mom says you're supposed to look after your little sister. But your little sister won't listen to a thing you say! Every time you tell her to do something, she says, "You can't make me! You're not my mother!"

Your mom needs to make it clear to your sister that you are in charge. Sit down with your mom and sister and talk about what your responsibilities really are. If you think your mom is expecting too much of you, let her know. If your sister thinks you have too much power, she also can let your mom know that. Together, you should be able to figure out a balance that works for both you and your sister.

Stuck Indoors

You and your brother are allowed to go to the park but only if you go together. Your brother never wants to do anything except play games on the computer. You don't think it's fair that you have to stay inside just because your brother won't budge.

Try making a deal with your brother. Maybe he will agree to half an hour of time outdoors if you'll take over a chore. And once you do coax him outside, who knows? He may have so much fun, he'll want to stay longer! If he still won't budge, talk the problem over with your parents. Together, you may be able to come up with some alternatives. Your parents may decide that they want your brother to spend more time outdoors, too. Or they may give you permission to go to the park with a friend.

Boredom Bickering

Your dad says that you and your sisters squabble because you can't find anything better to do. Well, he's right. There isn't anything better to do!

A little imagination can go a long way when you're hanging around with nothing to do. Put together a talent show for the other members of your family. If you're tired of checkers or Uno, create a new board game based on a book or movie you all like. Plan a special family feast—right down to the shopping list. Get a book of card games or magic tricks from the library, and challenge yourselves to learn one new game a week. Don't forget the fun-for-one activities on pages 48 and 49 of this book. What's fun for one is often even more fun with two or three!

Tattle Trouble

Your brother has a really bad temper. Whenever you don't do what he wants, he punches you or knocks you down. If you threaten to tell, he calls you a tattletale and a baby. You don't want to be a tattletale, but sometimes it hurts!

Here's a rule to go by: If anyone—no matter who it is—is hurting you, it's time to tell. That's not tattling. It's protecting yourself. Think of it this way: It's tattling if all you want to do is get somebody into trouble. It's not tattling if you help get someone out of trouble. Find a time when you can talk to a parent in private. If that doesn't help, find another adult you can trust. Your brother is being a bully, and he needs to be stopped.

Sibling-Saver Gadgets

Got sibling struggles? One of these relationship-saving devices can help:

- ## Headphones
  Your sister can't think without her favorite music, but you need complete silence to study. A set of headphones for your sister will solve this problem.

- ## Kitchen Timer
  Is one of you a phone or computer hog? Set a timer! When the buzzer sounds, it's time to get off.

- ## Memo Pad
  Got a gripe? Write it down on a pad of paper. If it's still important later, give the memo to your mom or dad and find a quiet time to discuss the situation.

kitchen basics

1. Follow the house rules for using appliances, knives, and other kitchen tools.

2. Wash your hands and scrub under your fingernails with soap and water before handling food. Keep washing until you've finished singing the "Happy Birthday" song twice.

3. Wipe up all spills as soon as they happen.

4. Put away food, rinse or wash all dishes, and wipe off the counter after you are finished.

i'm starving

Got an attack of the munchies? Grab a snack that's tasty and good for you, too. Before you start, make sure you know the kitchen basics. When you're ready to whip up something delicious, try these simple, no-bake ideas:

EZ Pizzas

These fresh pizzas need no baking. Spread cream cheese carefully onto a graham cracker. Decorate it with fresh fruit. Or try vegetable slices on wheat crackers.

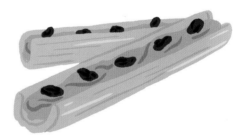

Crunchy Munchies

Make your own cheesy trail mix. Combine cheese crackers, rye chips, pretzel twists, and cracker sticks in a bowl. Mix together and munch away.

Ants on a Log

Wash celery sticks and pat them dry with a paper towel. Spread peanut butter on the celery and add raisins.

Veggie Sandwich

Make a salad sandwich. Spread veggie cream cheese on whole-grain bread. Layer with cucumber slices, tomatoes, and lettuce.

Deli Roll

Start with a romaine lettuce leaf. On top of it, layer a slice of lunch meat and a slice of cheese. Roll and eat!

sweet treats

Satisfy a sweet tooth with one of these yummy—and healthy—treats.

Waffle-wich

- Two whole-grain waffles
- Whipped topping
- Blueberries, raspberries, strawberries, or a mix

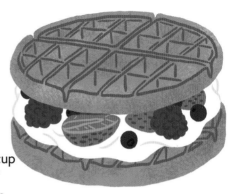

Toast both waffles until lightly browned. Top one waffle with ½ cup of whipped topping and ½ cup of berries. Place the second waffle on top.

Yogurt Pop

- Any flavor yogurt
- Plastic spoon

Open a small yogurt container, stick in a plastic spoon, and freeze overnight. The next day, dip the container into warm water, twist the spoon, and slide the container off. You've got a tasty yogurt pop.

Fruity Parfait

- Plain or vanilla yogurt
- Blueberries, raspberries, strawberries, or a mix
- Crispy rice cereal or granola

Layer plain or vanilla yogurt, berries, and cereal or granola in a bowl. Top it all off with more yogurt.

Choco-PB Popcorn

- Peanut butter
- Popcorn
- Sweetened cocoa powder
- Mini chocolate chips

Check with your parents to make sure it's ok to use the microwave when you're alone. Microwave 2 tablespoons peanut butter in a heat-safe bowl for 30 seconds. Pour 2 cups popcorn into a large bowl, and drizzle the melted peanut butter over the top. Mix in 2 teaspoons sweetened cocoa powder and 2 tablespoons mini chocolate chips.

Pineapple Fizz

- Pineapple juice
- Sparkling water

In a glass, mix ½ cup of pineapple juice and ½ cup of sparkling water. Stir gently.

Muffin Stack

- Bran muffin
- Chocolate-hazelnut spread
- Banana slices

Turn the muffin on its side on a cutting board. Use a butter knife to carefully slice the muffin into 3 layers. Separate the layers. Spread the chocolate-hazelnut spread and banana slices on each layer. Restack the layers.

key
thought

have fun

Being alone doesn't have to be boring.
Start a good book. Practice the piano.
Draw. String beads to make
a necklace. If you learn to make
the most of your time, it will
fly by quickly.

it's about time

Are you an early bird? Or do you believe in taking your sweet time? Pick the answers that best describe how you handle your time.

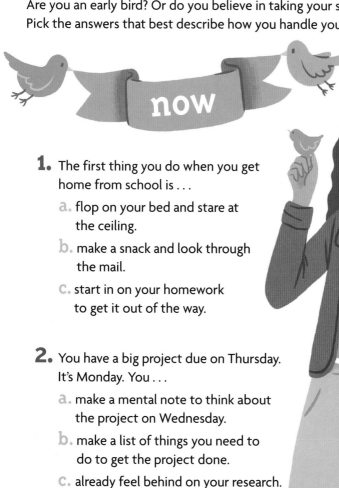

now

1. The first thing you do when you get home from school is . . .

   a. flop on your bed and stare at the ceiling.

   b. make a snack and look through the mail.

   c. start in on your homework to get it out of the way.

2. You have a big project due on Thursday. It's Monday. You . . .

   a. make a mental note to think about the project on Wednesday.

   b. make a list of things you need to do to get the project done.

   c. already feel behind on your research.

3. You're supposed to practice your trumpet 30 minutes every day. You . . .

   a. plan to practice an hour every other day instead—starting tomorrow.

   b. set a timer for 30 minutes at the beginning of your practice session.

   c. squeeze the 30 minutes in between soccer practice and Girl Scouts.

4. You and a friend are working on a class project together. You . . .

  a. tell her not to worry. You'll get your part of the project done—eventually.

  b. set up some times when you can get together and work on the project.

  c. finish your part of the project right away so that you can help her with her part.

5. You don't have enough time to finish your homework before dinner, so you . . .

  a. watch TV instead.

  b. start an assignment anyway so that there will be less to do after dinner.

  c. ask your mom if you can eat while you work.

6. If you could change the time you go to school, it would be . . .

  a. later, so that you could sleep longer in the morning.

  b. about the same.

  c. earlier, so that you could fit more activities into your day.

later

Answers

If you answered mostly a's, you like to take things slow and easy. People like being around you—you seem to have a knack for calming things down. Unfortunately, the rest of the world doesn't always work at your easygoing pace. You also may have a tendency to procrastinate, which means that things such as chores and schoolwork don't always get done on time.

Timely Tip: Hang a fun wall calendar in a place where you can't miss it. Jot down important activities and due dates. Then take a minute to check the calendar each day so that you don't get yourself into a bind. When you finish working today, write down what you plan to start tomorrow. You can also use a "reminder" application on your computer or smartphone to keep track of your to-do list.

On Time

If you answered mostly b's, you're usually on time, but you don't make a big deal about it. You like to keep an even pace and plan ahead when you need to. Your friends appreciate your common sense and know that they can count on you to get the job done.

Timely Tip: Got something super important to remember? Pin a reminder to your backpack. A bright button or ribbon will catch your eye. Use the same thing every time, and it'll jog your memory whenever you see it.

Ahead of Time

If you answered mostly c's, you are reliable and well organized and have a reputation for getting things done on time. You like to know what to expect and feel best when you have every-thing under control. Your friends sometimes call you a worrywart, but they admire how you stay on top of things.

Timely Tip: Make sure you don't leave having fun out of your busy schedule! At the beginning of the week, go over your calendar and find time each day that you can set aside for "doing nothing." Mark that spot with a sticker as a reminder that it's time to relax and enjoy!

fun for one!

Being alone means no interruptions and no distractions. So if you like to do something that requires privacy or total concentration, now's your time to do it.

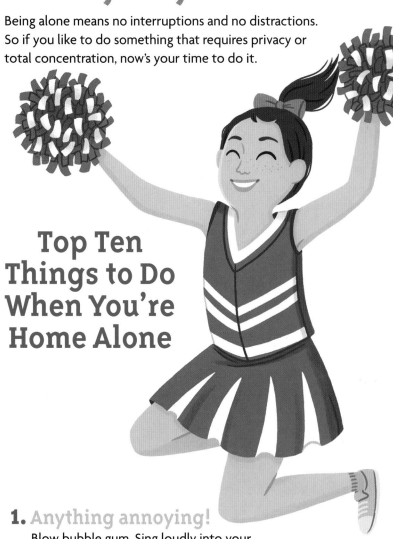

Top Ten Things to Do When You're Home Alone

1. Anything annoying!
Blow bubble gum. Sing loudly into your hairbrush. Practice a cheer over and over. Do whatever you love that others don't!

2. Write secrets in your diary.
No one will be around to peek over your shoulder.

3. Practice an instrument or a dance routine.
Being alone usually means you can make all the noise you want!

4. Become an expert.
Pick a subject you love and learn as much as you can about it.

5. Write a letter to a pen pal.

Use this time to keep in touch with your faraway friends.

6. Decorate your room.

Create a space you love to be in.

7. Read a novel.

Or pick up a pen and write a novel yourself!

8. Make a scrapbook.

Create a theme such as A Year in My Life, My Favorite Things, or My Summer Vacation. Fill your scrapbook with photos, drawings, newspaper clippings, ticket stubs—whatever tells your story.

9. Learn something new.

Use your time alone to develop a new skill. You'll find books at your local library on everything from juggling to origami.

10. Make a present.

Treat someone in your family to a special homemade gift. Creating the gift while that person's not at home will make it easy to keep it a surprise.

keep in touch

"Alone" doesn't have to mean "lonely." Here are some ways to connect with family and friends, even when they aren't around.

Keep a conversation journal.

Is there something you're just dying to tell your dad (or some-body else)? Jot it down in a journal or little notebook. Slip it in his briefcase along with a note asking for a response. Keep passing the notebook back and forth. You can carry on an entire conversation without speaking a word!

Start a virtual book club.

Make a plan with a friend or family member to read the same book at the same time. Decide how much of the book you will read at one time. Then arrange a phone call or e-mail time to chat about what you've read.

Pass notes.

Keep a daily journal with your friends. Fill it with doodles, jokes, thoughts, fortunes, fill-in-the-blank questions, and the latest news at school. Assign a day of the week to each friend. When it's your turn to take home the journal, you can respond to what the last person wrote. It's like passing notes in class—only you're writing at home, so you won't get into trouble! Surprise the next person in line with a special treat—tuck in stickers, a coupon, or a special cartoon to make her smile.

Send a friend a smile.

Whether your friend lives across the country or across the street, brighten her day with a handwritten letter or homemade card. Get creative by including drawings, puzzles, and fill-in-the-blank questions.

stay in control

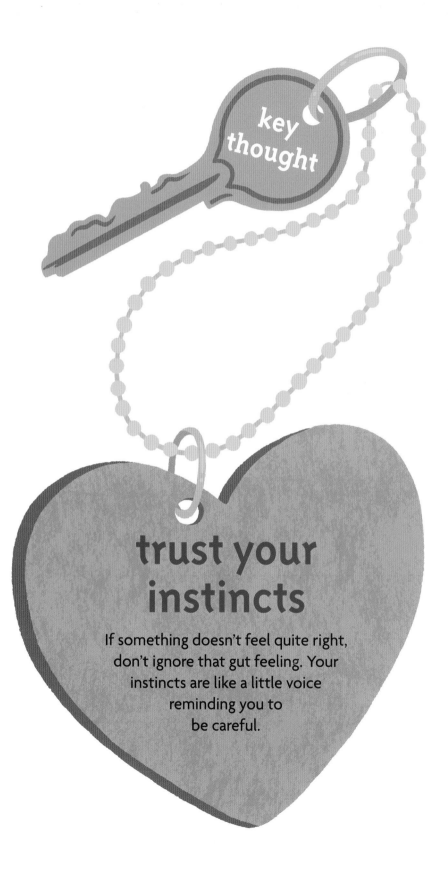

key
thought

trust your
instincts

If something doesn't feel quite right,
don't ignore that gut feeling. Your
instincts are like a little voice
reminding you to
be careful.

tricky situations

What do you do when you're not sure what to do? Trust your instincts!

Info Alert

Your friend just sent you a Web link for a project you're working on together. To see it, though, you have to enter your name and other personal information. Your mom and dad have said never to do that unless they OK the site first. But the only time your friend can work on the project with you is right now.

Your parents are right to insist that you don't enter personal information on a website without their permission. On a site that's not secure, Internet thieves can use that information to steal private data and even money from you or your parents. Ask your friend which parts of the site will be useful for your project. Then tell her you'll check it out after your parents get home.

Hold the Phone!

A woman on the telephone says she works with your dad. She wants to drop off some important papers for him to sign, but she forgot to get the address from him. If you'll give her your address, she'll bring the papers right by.

Something here doesn't make sense. If she works with your dad, why can't she get your address from his workplace, or better yet, leave the papers there? You know not to give out information over the telephone anyway. Tell the woman you'll have your dad or mom call her back.

The phone rings, but when you say "Hello," nobody answers. You're pretty sure it's a group of boys from your class making prank calls. They may be having fun, but you're not. And the calls are getting annoying.

It may just be a telemarketer, or it may be prankster kids you know. Either way, don't play along. When the phone rings again, don't answer it. If you have voicemail or an answering machine, let the caller leave a message. Chances are, the pranksters will get bored with their little game and quit calling. Let your parents know what's going on and that you won't be answering the phone. If the phone calls continue, talk over possible solutions to the problem with your parents.

Funny Feelings

You're practicing cartwheels in your front yard when you notice an unfamiliar van parked across the street. The driver is sitting behind the wheel, looking out the window. Come to think of it, the same van was parked in the same place yesterday.

There's no law against sitting in a parked car. Maybe the driver is just taking a break, but it's not up to you to figure that out. Something about that van is making you nervous. Follow that instinct. Go inside and lock the door behind you. Tell your parents about the van (or point it out if it's still there when they get home). Use the message pad by the phone to write down any information you remember.

Who's There?

You're sitting at the dining-room table doing your homework when you notice someone pass by outside. You sneak up to the window to get a better look, and you see a man next to the house!

Don't panic. This doesn't necessarily mean danger. During the day, a variety of service people can show up at your house—from a cable repairperson to the utility-meter reader. Most of the time, their work is done outside your house, and they won't come to your door. You might even see a service truck parked outside. So stay put, take a breath, and call your mom to let her know what's going on. If someone should ring the doorbell, it's best not to answer it, even if the person is wearing a uniform. Whoever it is can come back another time or leave a note for your parents. Let your mom and dad know someone came by, and they can look into it.

Relax!

Even if you're used to staying home alone, you might feel scared from time to time. If you think you're in danger, your heart beats faster, you take short breaths, and you start thinking scary thoughts. But if there is no real danger, then there is no reason for your body to work so hard. You can help to calm down by changing your thoughts or changing your inside body speed. It doesn't matter which one you do first, because the other one will just about always follow automatically.

To change your thoughts,
say things like these to yourself:

- I can think of an explanation for what just scared me, if I just try.
- I know my own house very well and I know where I feel safest inside.
- I can turn on the TV or radio to keep me company. I can also turn on lights all around the house so that it will seem like other people are home.

- My parents wouldn't leave me home alone if it wasn't safe.
- I've done all the things that I'm supposed to.
- I've done this before and I've been OK.

- If I were babysitting now, what would I tell a younger child who felt afraid?
- I have a backup plan that I worked out with my parents before I stayed alone the first time. I can always use it if I need to.

To slow down your heart rate and breathing, try this surprising tip:
- Do 20 jumping jacks or run in place for one minute. When you stop, your heart will slow down by itself and go back to normal.

what do you do?

Do you know what to do in an emergency? Babysitters' training courses such as the ones offered by the American Red Cross will teach you the basics. Some organizations, such as hospitals and YMCAs, offer classes just for kids who stay home alone. These tips will also help you stay in control:

1. **DO** know the emergency numbers for your community. Make sure the numbers are posted where you can easily find them in case of an emergency.

2. **DO** keep a flashlight and extra batteries in a place where you can always find them—even in the dark!

3. **DO** stay away from windows and glass doors if it's stormy outside.

4. **DO** know where you should go in case of severe weather. The safest places in most houses are the basement and a hall or closet near the center of the house.

5. **DO** use a battery-operated radio. Sometimes bad weather makes electricity go out, so a radio run on batteries can help you hear alerts about the weather.

6. DO leave the house and call 911 from a neighbor's house if you smell gas. It has a funny smell you may not be used to. Your parents can help you recognize it.

7. DO keep electrical appliances away from water every time you use them.

8. DO remember the most important thing to do in case of fire: Get out of the house. Do not stop to take anything with you. Practice using escape routes with your parents, and talk to them about getting your pets out safely.

9. DO make like a snake and crawl along the floor if you are in a room filled with smoke.

10. DO stop, drop, and roll if any part of your clothing catches fire.

ouch!

Need an adhesive bandage—or more? When you're on your own, you must rely on your first-aid know-how. The best way to get that information is by attending a first-aid or babysitting class offered by your local hospital or the American Red Cross. If you get hurt and don't know what to do, call your doctor's office or 911. Use these guidelines to help you take care of yourself and decide if you need to call for help.

Sprained or Twisted Ankle

- Place ice in a ziplock bag and wrap in a towel. Apply the cold pack to your ankle for about 20 minutes.

- Lie down to rest.

- Keep your ankle raised on the arm of a chair or a pillow so that your ankle is higher than the rest of your body.

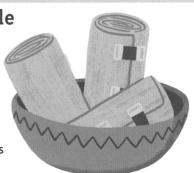

Nosebleeds

- Sit down, and lean your head forward.

- Pinch the soft part of your nose to squeeze the nostrils closed until it stops bleeding.

- If your nose is still bleeding, try pinching it again. If that doesn't help, call your parent or 911.

Choking

- Make a fist with the thumb side against your belly, just above your belly button.

- Grab the fist with your other hand.

- Thrust or quickly pull your fist up and into your belly.

- Repeat until whatever you're choking on pops out of your mouth. Call 911 and then your parents.

Fever

- If you think you have a fever, call a parent.
- Drink cool, clear liquids (water or juice).
- DON'T take any medicine without first getting permission from a parent.

Cuts

- Press a clean cloth on the cut to stop the bleeding.
- Wash the cut with soap and warm water.
- Cover with an adhesive bandage.
- Call a parent or 911 if the wound is serious.

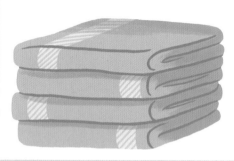

Poisoning

- If you mistakenly swallow anything that isn't food, call the poison control center or 911 immediately.
- Tell the operator what you swallowed, and follow his or her directions carefully.
- Don't take any medicine unless the operator tells you to.

Burns

- Immediately put the red area under cold—not icy—running water for at least five minutes.
- If the burn is large, white, or bleeding, call 911.
- Don't put anything on the burn—not even a bandage.
- If the burn still bothers you, call a parent.

Bee or Wasp Stings

- Scrape the stinger off with your fingernail, a card, or another stiff item.
- Wash the sting with soap and water.
- Press ice or a cold compress on the area to reduce the pain and swelling.

good for you!

key
thought

relax—you're
in control

You know what it takes to be cool-
headed and confident when
you're home alone. Why?
You know someone you can
really count on—YOU!

need-to-know info

Have the right information at the moment you need it. Here is a place to keep track of important info and house rules. Talk with your parents to fill in the blanks, and then tear out the booklet and put it in a handy spot.